THE BONE WEIR

The Bone Weir

D.S. Stymeist

*For Lynn, Love your work.
Thanks so much for coming
to Ottawa.*

*In Solidarity
David*

fhp Frontenac House Poetry

Book design: Neil Petrunia, Epix Design
Cover Image: Tim Nokes
Author photo: Phillipa Maitland

Library and Archives Canada Cataloguing in Publication

Stymeist, D. S., 1967-, author
        The bone weir / D.S. Stymeist.

Poems.
Issued in print and electronic formats.
ISBN 978-1-927823-55-2 (paperback).–ISBN 978-1-927823-56-9 (pdf).–
ISBN 978-1-927823-57-6 (html)

        I. Title.

PS8637.T96B65 2016   C811'.6   C2016-904126-3
                                             C2016-904127-1

Frontenac House gratefully acknowledges the support of the Canada Council for
the Arts for our publishing program. We would also like to thank the Government
of Alberta Multimedia Development Fund for their support of our publishing
program.

 Canada Council **Conseil des Arts**
for the Arts **du Canada**   *Alberta* Government

Printed and bound in Canada
Published by Frontenac House Ltd.
1648 Bowness Road N.W.
Calgary, Alberta, T2N 3J9, Canada
Tel: 403-263-7025

www.frontenachouse.com

for Sara and Julia

Table of Contents

Artifact: The Levellois Point

This stone flake still cuts as sharp
as thirty-thousand years ago.

Unearthed in a Paris suburb, it reveals
the apex of Neanderthal cousins' craft.

If we descend far down the spiral
coil of our genealogical scale,

we come from stone stock, Neolithic
workers in crypo-crystaline mineral.

Once, this knapper of rock draped
a caribou hide over bent knee

to chip out an oval-shaped ring
from hunk of chert stone, forming

a circuit of scars, and with deft
clip shear off a flake that looks

surgical and modern, but isn't.
It chills to dig and tear open

the ground that lies between us,
for like a swift runner who loses

by margin of a leaf's breadth,
this point, despite the look of skill

and sapience, proves less durable,
less certain, than our own work;

and that small gap, that separation
proved their undoing and our making.

Extinct Americana: Miracinonyx, The American Cheetah

In the history of American fauna
you were built for sudden haste,
for the short burst across prairie flat
to drag down your fleeing prey:
the rocket cars on Bonneville salt
a distant echo of your swift tempo.

Crossing the plain south of Battleford
a herd of pronghorn kick up the dust
as they start over lines of barbed wire
and bound away. Despite alarm
in the pits of their eyes, nothing
alive can now chase them down.
Were they spooked by some ghost
called up from grassland bone-yard?

Pictographic

Every year it becomes harder
to locate the old red image
amid rock cap moss and lichen.
Hazy, pale, and eroding away,
it has become a rusty smudge.

The canoe sways in waves,
yet we need to find stillness
to pick out the faded design.
Then the pictogram's peculiar
rabbit ears pop up as if
it jumped clear of cover.

Your ears still mark you.
Company men once thought
the sharp spurs satanic horns,
named the place Devil's Lake,
and barred their Cree guides
from setting up camp onshore.

That familiar rhythm of place,
return after return, was broken.
But don't your ears still perk up
with interest on hearing your name,
We-sakejak. Great Hare, con-man,
trouble-maker, fool, and our hero.

When people first built canoes,
who fashioned their paddles?
Was it then that ears sprouted,
became blades of seaplanes?

When crossing at night,
after wind has passed over
and stars spread on water,
you hide there, silent,
crouching in pitted granite,
still waiting for steady hands
to retouch fading colours,
to refresh hushed blood.

Ghost Gardens of Detroit

South of Detroit-Hamtramck Assembly
lies the forgotten rectangle of Perrien Park.
The pattern, laid-out during days of Arts
& Crafts, shows prescience: a large X,
a crossed-out census form box,
a man spread-eagled, staked to ground.

Like the beast totems and burial mounds
of Ohio, this emblem was meant to be seen
from airless space and signifies the excised
expectations of this onetime Emerald Oz.

Now, the city's closed fifty-seven parks,
and none dare day-stroll the east-side.
The skinny, ragged crews of crack-
heads abandon the wild streets
as urban desolation turns to ruin.

Along Forest and Grandy, grass
grows between blocks of pavement —
it's hard to keep to the sidewalk
as it crumbles into broken chunks.

In front of a pile of bricks, day-lilies
spread wealth of solid 24 ct. gold.
Between oaks, a stand of rhubarb
gone to seed. You can still trace
the ghost rows of a backyard garden.

A single standing house endures,
the windows grease-stained,
but unbroken. An old hand pulls back
the curtain, looks out with suspicion.
All his neighbours ran off, or died.
The city has gone belly-up, no more
refuge of labour, no more beacon
for storm-broken, dispossessed.

Misi-Ginebig (lake-serpent)

I.

Embroiled in bad dreams, a serpent
lies beneath folds of mercury.
It shudders and rolls right over,
driving the lake into a cauldron
of white caps, scud, and froth.
We won't check the nets today;
those silver flashes on waves
are clear signs of malevolence.

Since water turned inside out,
flow damned, current reversed
to drive force into the hydro-turbines
of Kettle, Limestone, and Long Spruce,
the neglected spirits of under lake
bloat — become greasy and unkind.
While poplars shudder in chorus,
lice and contagion line the gill-slits.

II.

As we haul up
the gill-net, a black Mariah-fish
spills out and writhes over wood
strakes leaving a splatter and trail
of fish slime.

Lacustrine eelpout:
her lower barbell a lone sixth string
of guitar, a whip-cord, a false stinger;
she's a deep, sly one and rarely seen.
We're pulling a string of nets behind
an island, near where a Caterpillar
fell through soft ice, a weak spot
the driver should have seen.

In spring, crows found him,
his rotten flesh an orange peel
soaked in oil. But the fishing's good,
unlike much of the lake. Shoals
of whitefish, walleye, and lake trout
now vanished. Loss traded for
influx of carp and red sucker.

On the way back to fish camp,
we speed past Long Point tents.
The Spences lost one of their girls
off the dock a few weeks earlier,
young Dora, never a strong swimmer,
dragged under by pull of current,
fished out the following day, beached
on the planks. Now her marker
flashes whitely with fresh paint.
Her brothers refuse to swim.

III.

Like flying in a dream — float
over the drowned beaches
that youth once made love on.

Like flying in a dream — drift
among rusted-out Cherokees,
Broncos, water tanks, and school-buses

that litter the bottom of lake.

IV.

Clothed in tire treads, shopping bags,
discarded bottles, the split-tongued
horror daubs on warrior paint,
smearing sulfur, nitric acid over lips,
cheeks, forehead, over implated curves
of scale; it tenses coiled force
to spring free the sudden ambush.

Chauvet Man

At Chauvet, our ancestors came
to limn with charcoal and ochre
the spirits of wild beasts
killed, skinned, consumed:
the hunger of our flesh that fed
on rich marrow and gore.

On the cave wall, a woolly rhino
cuts a comic figure on stone
with its floppy, saggy folds of hide,
and myopic, minimal eyes.

All across the glacial plains
of Scythia, Gallica, and Mercia
this short-sighted, short-tempered
brute became the grudging butt
for our talent for legerdemain.

In the inner depths of the chalk
cave, their bones lie scattered;
here, ghosts greet others of kind,
those mega-fauna of ice age,
who slouched their massy ways
off to an animal necropolis.

Last Night

In Barcelona, where shadows linger
in the corners and avenues run wide,
we spent our final days and nights.

Caught in the halo of street lamp
cast through open shutters,
your body glowed on the bed.

You, moon-faced, white cheeked,
tossing your lank hair back like
the mane of a Dakota mare.

Your thighs, ripe winter melons,
softly pliant under thrust and pull —
our rude copy of Picasso's rude

painting of a bull-man astride
his Ariadne that we'd seen earlier
on the stone of gallery walls.

With hardening breast and ring
your body worked against mine
— we used everything we knew.

When we lay back on the sheets,
we could hear, in the far distance,
the rumble of uncoupling freight.

One last, familiar gesture of hand
running over loose curl of hip and flank,
and then dark, sugared embrace of sleep.

Although we met time to time,
it did not matter, for that night
was when we said our farewell.

Does the stone bear in the plaza
still eat his mountain honey,
careless of the stinging bees?

The 401 Series

1.

Filling psychotic sky with drone,
machinery speeds ceaselessly
down endless circuit of highway —
the terror never sleeps, never rests.
All peripheral understanding cut off
by drivers' blind need to projectile
into future, to move into stream,
spin generator of hive's hum-song.

2.

Just as red corpuscles jet sweet O_2
through net of arteries and veins
to fire-up and stoke cellular combustion,
a freeway swarm of cars, school-buses,
semi-trailers, postal vans, fire trucks,
armored cars, floral delivery vans,
and endless variation of *just in time*
conveyances circulate tackle and gear
from one serpentine end to other.
If life consists of jive and incessant
coupling, then this juggernaut
is much more fully alive than I.

3.

Think not that you remain you
when behind the driver's wheel.
I've seen chamber maids, pastry
chefs, curtain salesmen overcome —
thoughtless, impulsive, consumed
by mind-rage of beltway and byway.

4.

Like the harrowing towers of Manhattan
that dwarf spectators into insignificance,
this hub of millionoid mass-transit
makes me entirely besides the point.
Am I appendix? An anachronistic organ
of this organism, nervously awaiting
the inevitability of appendectomy?

5.

Through ranks of merging lanes
a maddening contagion flares,
impelling drivers to precipitously gasp
as they join the explosive force of piston,
rubber, gasoline that rolls over blank
circuit of dun-coloured pavement.

6.

A man with bared teeth shuffles along
asphalt; his dreads flap in smutty wind
as his Ford Fiesta alights in the passing
lane. The greasy smoke of diesel fire
boils up into the miasma-obscured sky,
a sacrificial offering of charred bones.
And behind blockage, traffic builds,
cars and emergency vehicles crushed
into immobile regiments that spew
exhaust through open mouths.

7.

As doped-up oracles of Delphi inhaled
toxic smoke belched from inmost Dis,
I can not avoid breathing this opioid fog.
When the Four-O-One speaks to me
with maggoty tendrils of crosstown transit,
it tongues an advert fresh and cherry ripe:
"Gain insight through amputation."

8.

And —, —, — it all! Ahead
brake-lights flare in an uneven row
as rubber-necking drivers slow
and trigger an unholy chain of near-
collisions and panicked squeals.
Breathe deep and recite prayer:
"Aum Namah Shiva."

                         Hold on and hope!

9.

Now we're all blocked up, backed up,
with nowhere to go, it's the nightmare
of Santa Monica Xpressway all over again,
except Dorothy isn't in the States no more.
And look around — a chemical implosion
behind drivers' starting rabbit eyes:
Good god! They're raving, blind, insane.

10.

Can anything live in wasteland of steel,
concretion, and layers of crushed stone?
The infernal motor-drone, day in, day out
is inimical to the life and breath biotic,
and drives unfortunates who press up
against the cemented honeycombs
to cast away the crumbs of longing.

11.

And, I can't believe it, we're moving again.
Oh sweet freedom! Oh sweet delight!
The open liberation of road gapes
before me as great flying beasts
wing their goony ways into Pearson
to cast jumbo shadows over macadam.

12.

Earlier, on Bellamy roadway,
a street-poor, gutter punk knew
that this hum was not idle thrum:
"Listen to what's below, buddy.
Listen to the throb, the gasp, the groan.
Listen to planet being ground down."

13.

The volume of traffic swells once more
with a foul burst of tinplated vinyl
speeding through alleys of collision;
an Astro-van shears across my lane,
its rear windows duck-taped shut
with garbage bags that ripple in the blast.

14.

To my right, a concrete mixer, huge, squat
as a mobile bunker, jigs up and down
on lubricated shocks like machine obscenity.
Oh, I'm disgusted, but my lawless eyes
are drawn back again and again,
to that jiggling, wiggling transom.

15.

Insomniacs of Markham, Pickering, Ajax,
can you hear this banshee's scream?
Can you hear her gag on her own effluvia,
in one final spasm of auto-erotic asphyxia?
"Choke me off, honey, choke me off."

16.
And now we're all going fast, fast, fast —
moving freely now, making good time.
The edges of pavement blur with speed,
and my slurred speech becomes drunkenly,
and I feel not at all one with the road,
but veer on edge of loss of control
towards convulsion, blood clot, and stroke.

17.
Is this it, buddy, is this your life?
this parade of shit boxes roaring past,
a stampede of glittering metal logos
on candy-coated hoods of cars.
more emblem than human being,
long ago consumed by commercial
fakery, seduced by the siren call
of Barracuda, Sunfire, Comet!

Anne Greene: 1650, Oxford

Anne greets visitors from her coffin.
They've come to finger lines of ligature
around her neck. They ask what she saw
and heard, but she does not answer.
All she remembers is darkness, choking pain.
Her father takes coins into his hands —
they still owe the doctors for blood letting.

Despite taunts mocking "the goatish flow
of her veins," Anne walks the lanes with neck
exposed, for her recovery from the noose
vindicates her from stain of child murder.

"Let scholars scoff in their Latin and Greek,"
she says, "for people that day saw the hand
of God." They separated her from earth,
alienated her from what gave her strength,
but she found a way to get back on her feet,
bound her wounds, buried her accusers.

River People

We're out along river banks
to escape airless suffocation,
rooms rented by the week.

Cans of domestic beer
line six-pack coolers,
sardines packed into tin.

A man holds his drink loosely,
wears the blank look that comes
from watching the river.

I'd strike up a conversation,
share my thermos of wine,
but know the value of silence.

Chief Snake's Funeral Catalogue

Bruises blackening with sunrise,
Chief Snake lay on stone
cobbles of a Kingston street.

Blankets: Fifteen One Point, Fifteen One &
a Half Point, Ten Two Point, Ten Two
and a Half Point, Ten Three Point.

Robinson and the boys
whooping it up on
Bahamian rum when
they came upon their man.

Fifty Yards of Broad Cloth, One Hundred
Yards of Calico, Seventy-Five Yards of
Callimanco, and Fifty-One Yards of
Cadies Silk.

Snake had filled the ears
of their company elder,
stoked this man's fear
for the men's jeopardy,
the peril of soul's fire.

A Dozen Ivory Combs. Twelve Pieces
of Gartering. Ten Common Guns.

Thus Snake counseled,
the elder barred — under pain
of lash — their country visits
to the Mississauga camps
to carouse with native girls.

Seventy-Two Fishing Hooks. Six Lined Hats
& Six Unlined Hats. One Hundred Pounds
of Gunpowder. A Dozen Hoes.

The coroner declared
Snake's death murder.
Then, certain of soldiers'
conviction, Gov. Simcoe
prepared pardons in secret.

> *Ninety Pounds of Brass Kettles. Three*
> *Dozen Butcher Knives. One Hundred Yards*
> *of Linen.*

It was just "a drunken brawl,"
the troopers pled at trial.

> *Two Dozen Cod Lines, Thirty Six*
> *Mackerel Lines.*

When the Cameronians
were let off, scot-free,
the Mississauga gathered
to thrust towards Montreal.

> *Fifty Yards of Molton Felt. Five Hundred*
> *Sewing Needles.*

From Manitoulin they came,
from shores of Great Lakes,
for the death-debt unpaid,
atonement in blood or goods,
for *ishpaginzo*. They'd pay
the price or suffer vengeance.

Fifty Yards of Embossed Serge, One piece
50 yards of Black Strouds,
and the same of Blue.

Thus pressed, the colony supplied
a state funeral for Chief Snake.
The offerings were items of utility,
service, and perhaps delight,
gifts from a dead man to his people.

Twelve Pounds Vermillion. A Dozen Looking Glasses.
One Hundred Pounds of Tobacco.

The Sanitarium Garden

At St. Remy he resided
with other madmen.

The flat of brush applied
over and over, building up
pattern of distortion and wave.
Trees move in this wind,
they shudder and rumba
as if ensnared by spirit.
Leaves, red and gold,
float up into seething sky.
The dark-green cedar
narrows, pointing to flight.

Two ill-proportioned trunks,
ugly jade-purple, snake up
the painting: bars that hold
us in and frame garden fires.

Riverbank

Running along the stream edge
is a lip of ice the river licks at
ceaselessly — labial, smooth, and dripping.
And thus, drop by drop, the steady work
of a moist tongue melts ice away.

Skyline

A howling yowl runs along Jasper
as road-signs clank on pavement.
Opening shop, a man braves the wind;
it begins to keen with sharper wail.

The flexured echo of mirrored panels
causes a skyward look: last week
the westerly stream left two dead,
entombed in collapse of scaffolding.

While earth's edge has swallowed sun,
magenta and azure waves ripple across
metrical sequence of reflective squares —
the high-gloss cubism of urban geometry.

Up there, rivulets of sky-light play at tip
and summit of these synthetic peaks
as subterranean rush-hour channels by
with tenebrous flood of chrome and rubber.

The Cheddar Gorge Skulls

We stripped flesh from bone
and ate the dead at Gough cave;
we turned decapitated heads
into cups. This was not a loving act.
We buried our own with care.

This skull craft affirms our humanity,
the ingenuity of your stone age
progenitors, who once crossed
the sunken lands of the Channel
to travel northward to Somerset.

We followed wake of glacial retreat,
sought to drive horse and caribou
off the Mendip hills into the gorge.
We grabbed stone mauls, knocked
off jawbones and lower orbitals,
scalped entire faces, features and all.
We took flint with finger and thumb,
scraped away clotted human hair.

With crude precision, we rapped
shafts of antler to rough out rim-edge,
to shape makeshift bowls for wine
brewed of wild grape. What cheer
that brought us, what chill dispelled.

Tibetan monks drink from silvered
cups of skull to remind themselves
of life's impermanence and fragility.
But not us. No, your forgotten
fathers spurned priestly ways,
we watchful, barefaced realists
cracked and cut fraternal bones
to suck marrow before discarding
the rest on a heap of waste-not.

Some say savage, brute. Not I.
We instead say, we too of bloody rite
took familiar parts, found our places
and raised the strange weight of crown
to toast our lives, such as they were.

Naked

When she disrobes, there comes
a sudden unfolding, a dilation,
for her body is slip-thin, delicate
as ermine, martin, or winter mink.

Yet her sight glisters with grief.
Apt augurs of uncertain endings,
those Geatish weather-eyes only
too well spot the shifting, faithless ways
of my *amour,* tell her which fruits
shall ripen and which shall not.

Big Rock (Okotoks, Alberta)

Easy to believe, that Big Rock,
now lying on grassland with back
broken, once rolled and chased
first man, trickster, and rodeo clown.

Everyone agrees Napi had it coming.
After all, he stole that buffalo hide,
he just didn't think Old Man Rock
would get off his fat ass and chase.

Mankind's chums, Deer and Antelope,
tried to help. Okotoks wouldn't listen.
Outraged, Old Man Rock, churned
right over them, leaving erratic trail

of quartzite dust and tumbleweed.
Rock rolled closer and closer,
as man chugged across the plain.
The bull-bats proved last hope;

they dive-bombed hurtling rock
till faces were bashed-in flat.
At last, spiteful stone broke,
tumbled to sudden, final stop.

Okotoks hasn't moved since.
He just sits and stares out
at the wavering line of horizon,
an old man sitting on his porch.

Yeah, they named a brewery
after me. Still, it'd be really nice
if someone threw me a blanket.
It gets cold out here in the wind.

Solitary

Lonely in your basement rental
      Cooking for one,
A glass by bottle of wine,
        The red element aglow.

Driving through night,
        With work in the dawn.
The lights are all green,
        There's no reason to stop.

A chill rises from the river,
        You don't tremble,
Your body warm under rain,
        Your breath a puff of vapor.

Faceless

With two thunderous blasts of sea-horn,
the ungainly steel bulk of luxury-liner
wallows into port to loom over Castries
like an overfed and dyspeptic moon-calf.

Out of our solariums, pleasure domes,
discotheques, coffee bars, sea-water pools
with full bar service, and all-you-can eat
buffets, we disgorge onto concrete pier

in an extended gout of tan and khaki
cruise-wear. The St. Lucia tourist
board girls, dressed in scanty flashes
of shrill colour, shimmy black hips

to the calypso beat of dockside band.
Everyone puts on their very best face
to greet the featureless stream that pushes
by on way to barter for tourist trinkets.

Despite long exposure to the dogged
tide of tourist flow, locals still look
unsettled by the sun-bleached shades
who leave small coins behind in their wake.

Reclamation

At the end of a dirt road that runs
in and out of olive and cedar groves,
past fields of wheat-stock stubble,
you come upon Sant'Antimo abbey.
Within its tartar-stained, grey walls
lie odd fragments of older stone:
half-way up the square block-tower
is a roman toilet carved of blue-veined
marble and stuffed with rough cobbles.
Around the corner, a toga-garbed figure
carries a basket of summer grapes
among the dressed blocks of travertine.
Salvaged from a nearby Roman villa,
this stone man has come up in the world
and has the best view of the Val d'Orcia.

That these fragments of old masonry
now cloister relics of Saint Anthimus,
who smashed Faunus' simulacrum
and was thrown into river Tiber
with a millstone clapped round neck
for his crime, is an irony unapparent
to the canons regular who chant
the Gregorian in gleaming white.

When midnight comes and dogs
pull my body apart, I can only hope
that the busted-up and unhallowed
remains of ill-used life will serve
in ways beyond my intention.

Bitterskin's Curse

She came to Scarborough bluffs
to watch the *Speedy* flounder by;
in sorrow, spirit sharp against all,
Bitterskin jigged her witch-dance.

Her son, Ogetonicut, held captive
on a green-timbered schooner
bound for Newcastle: the trilling
of wood ducks filling his dreams.

At Scugog, he'd knifed John Sharp,
a fur-trader and whiskey man.
Enraged at brother's death, he paid
the debt with this stranger's blood.

The schooner, taking on water,
struggled in October nor'easters.
Square-sailed, sluggish, forced to tack
its listless way along lake shore.

Off Presqu'ile, a squalling blizzard
left the crew groping purblind
to both star-fix and shore-fire,
left to sail by magnetic needle alone.

The lake bed anomalous, mesmeric,
drawing the iron point of compass
twenty-two degrees from true north,
charming the ship towards doom.

There, a bare half-fathom below,
the jut of Devil's Hitching Post
rent and tore hull asunder
and sent the brigantine down.

With dawn, the compass box,
a few broken-up poultry coops,
and a mast cracked in half
washed up on western shoal.

Firm in conviction that men
from little York had drowned,
Bitterskin ceased dancing,
turned her back to the shore.

The Gillnetters

In the grey hour, rubber boots
champ over gravel; torn nets
hang from red willow like webs —
they wait for more patient hands.

At the end of rain-slicked dock,
the boatman glares; it's high time
to be on the water, time to world's
edge where our nets hang.

Freshwater yawlers learn the trade
by eye; words rarely passed lips
of the boatman: either you knew
what was what or were useless.

Head and foot ropes skate over
the prow gunwale as we haul in.
From tangled, twisted seine,
we work to pry free our catch.

Gasping in unwelcome air,
they come to line blue tubs;
a fin, a five spot, slides through
my hands back underwater.

With the slip of rounded blade,
the work of gutting begins —
glide behind gill and then down
the line of snow-white, soft belly.

The boatman opens a pike,
and whitebait, half-swallowed
into their spirit world, spill onto
the gutting board like new birth.

Elemental

Your body is what I wish to unravel
with all the carnal presence of touch.
With the coming of dusk, I begin
to smooth that blond that spreads
across your swimmer's shoulders.
I trace pebbled ridges of corona
with the tips of fingers, grasp
the spoils of berry-ripe nipples.
To brush the honey-combed topaz
that burnishes skin, to stroke
the wet, sex-bewitched slit that lies
between your upraised hips
is to reach for all that is tangible.

Pinhole Man

At Pinhole Cave, another grotto pun:
a crook-backed man with erect penis
scrimshawed haphazardly onto
the side of a thick slab of rib —
the hard bone, mammalian armor,
now playfully turned to an *après dine*
canvas where in thin cartoonish lines
a lone dancer carouses in his mask.
Our liminal Adam, first root and seed,
and all that untimely, unimagined woe
to the woolly, hairy beasts of the field.

Crush

When she held me tight and crushed
       her chubby paps against my chest,
I could hardly breathe much less speak.
       Her lips, pearled with *Manitoba Mavin*,
she brought to mine with a wet smack.
       With a mawkish mien she whispered
of a later that night *voulez-vous*
       at the cabin beside the short-haul rapids.
Suzy had stormed in with her girl-pals,
       those wise-cracking, slavering punkettes
who pirated away all my whiskey and gin,
       and fled back out into the summer's night
while she held me down with her lip-lock.

Sunken

As we breached waves at Mazatlan,
my father's arm supported me.
Out in the bay, our twinned shadows
startled a school of Crevalle jacks,
made them flee between coral.

He'd caught the gleam of something
and dived below. When he reappeared
he held a corroded knife in his fist.

On land, he recounted the cruelty
of East German swim coaches
at high-school, those brutalities
waged across America to bridge
a gap in arms.

           Next summer,
I cut myself on that dull blade,
and my father's anger surfaced.

After stitching the wound shut,
the doctor told me not to run barefoot
on beach, to watch for buried glass;
she couldn't number the feet she'd sewn.

Our Language

Composed of spittle, glower, and bark,
our language was not meant to dance
to the melodic lines of *uccelli canterini.*
No, it was bred of a core of urban rot
for thrust, counter, and right-cross.

To increase our treasure of discord
we have chivied out and hijacked
the word-hoards of other tongues —
the still-wet trophies of hunters' skill.

And Cheers! to my fellow sailors,
press-ganged and *pi mal,* flung to sea
to run amuck in foreign ports of call
and become the marks of wise-assed
punks, the *khn rak* of street courtesans.

All that dealing, contracting, and briskly
trading our virulent lexical poxes
for those of Kalicut, Naples, and Bataam,
all that priceless cargo to feed
an appetite for pepper and spice.

When we've tongued and swallowed
enough of the gob-smacking gobbets
of our beloved, despised, mongrel argot
we quicken and heave forth our words.

Peregrine

With last days of spring, the walk
over the Highlevel unsettles;
bird carcasses litter roadside —
hapless tufts of feather and bone
washed into the rain-gutters,
the dark rinds of flesh resinous,
like catacombed holy men of Evora.

All at once, an omen appears:
four wings beating together as one,
linked in horror like forced coital act,
a sight not meant for human eyes.
The bird's talon hooks sink deep
into crop of shock-struck pigeon.
As it flutters, spins, twists, and turns,
the greater pulse of pinion and gear
sweeps it along city-canyon walls.

The peregrine's scream turns
children at play to stone, its lone
expressive syllable honed sharper
than gull-winged Stuka's drop over
the war-torn ghettos of Warsaw.

The falcon wings its way straight up
to tall concrete of corporate tower
and high-rise urban condominium,
banking away from abyss of erasure,
a survivor of toxic alchemy.

The Snow Bed

Curled up as if asleep, Lola
lay in a bank of drifted snow.
Kiss of hoarfrost dappled cheeks,
lips, and lids. She never spoke —
swampy-eyed, always on verge
of flight. Tired of our tomfoolery,
tired of rye, bonfire, Lola found
a bed. Now ravens hop all around.

Tree Lobster
(Dryococelus australis)

Down to your last two dozen,
you sought the shade of a melaleuca,
one that hung off the edge of world.

Carried from Eden to the sea stack
of Ball's Pyramid in unsuspecting beak,
Sticky walked away from bird's nest.

The second miracle of parthenogenesis,
where males become only optional,
did the rest of the work of regeneration.

For nine decades the sterile basalt jut
of volcanic caldera proved unlikely ark
for this huge and flightless phasmid.

When the *Makambo* ran aground
on Ned's Beach, black rats escaped
and infested your home world.

Before songs of rain-bird and fantail
were gone, Howe Islanders missed you:
they liked to bait hooks with your bodies.

Now 20,000 amphora-shaped eggs
await in the crypts of Melbourne zoo
for the poisoning of your enemies.

Homecoming

By me he fell, by me he died
  ~ Aeschylus' Oresteia.

She rubbed oil through his tangled
locks, and the scale of passage
over the ocean-sea washed away.
The men were drunk, singing war songs.
Women's laughter echoed in the night.
Was is it her eyes, or did the shadows
that sat in the corners begin to rock?

The coarse, dark hair of his chest
reminded her of the Calydonian boar
dead at the point of her lance.
With tips of her fingers, she traced
the broken map of pallid cicatrix
that wormed underneath skin.

His head began to nod and loll.
Keen and well-loved, the blade
felt heavy; its weight reminded her
of how his cock had felt in her hand.
Slow poison would've been easy,
but she would not have it said
she took a woman's way out.

She placed the tip under shoulder
blade and shanked between ribs —
he woke as life-blood spilled out,
staining the bath waters purple.

The Wanderer

As the condor wings its way across
the mountain rim of Sierra Madre,
it circles and rises with the thermals,
seeking out the smell of rot on wind.

Where have those days of plenty gone?

The black sable boa flung around
bony, hunch-backed shoulders
chicly frames the angular features
and raw, red eyes of this brood
aristocrat of the strato-cumuli.

Somewhere behind bloodshot glint
lie memories of how strong-backed
beasts drifted down valley highways
to ditch their bodies for bird's delight.

In those days, kin and kind would geier
and kettle like giants in the bruised deep
over carcasses of wooly mammoth
and mastodon. They'd black-out
the sky over the fallen and sun-fattened.

Gathering in wakes they rejoiced
that sharp cut of scimitar beak
into rawhide to make a slick,
deep hole into which to slither
naked neck and pluck out gobbets.

She now finds herself brawling
with mobs of common vultures
over the tatty remains of rabbit
exposed by sun and snowmelt.

Where have those days of feasting gone?

When I Have the Body of a Wolf

After Elizabeth Bachinsky, "When I have the body of a man."

When I have the body of a wolf,
I'm ten feet tall and lope through the dark.

When I'm ten feet tall and lope through the dark,
Lock up your daughters, hold your loved ones tight.

When you lock up your daughters, hold your loved ones tight,
I'll lick my wounds till they bleed freshly.

When I lick my wounds till they bleed freshly,
I'll sharpen my teeth the better to eat you with.

When I sharpen my teeth the better to eat you with,
I can smell the sex on your skin and hair.

When I can smell the sex on your skin and hair,
My appetite begins to gore me with its horn.

When my appetite begins to gore me with its horn,
I look for the living among the dead.

When I look for the living among the dead,
I'll have the body of a wolf.

Keewatin

When suicide came for mother,
the bitch just slipped in under
the door on one of those nights
when lake wolves became silent
but the blizzard kept howling.

She came in the guise of medicine,
offered an arsenal of painkillers,
a pharmacopia of lotus and soma
— drugs to calm clawing doubt,
cease incessant acts of self-wounding.

Was this seduction not to be resisted,
an embrace never broken, never
betrayed? Only the prying force
of others, the efficacy of stomach
pumps began to loosen that grip.

Then, when young ones came,
they said that you couldn't leave.
Now when a storm blows itself out,
silence echoes, clear and clean,
like running water, like a river.

Water-Birds on the Rideau

Over the gravel, water runs,
a serpent, a cormorant snaps
after fry that dart in the shallows.

Mid-stream, on limestone crag,
another dark bird perches,
cleans dank and oily feathers,
bends into a figure of sibilance.

The hooked claw, scaled web,
blue-green glass of bird's eye
conceal ancient saurian craving
for alteration and skin-change —
to free self from elemental bonds.

Mischief Lake Bear

The bear came at night to steal
fish. In the morning, paw prints
crisscrossed the muddy ground.

When the hollow-point struck,
sudden pain surprised her.
As if she were a dying samurai,
she reared to face us — urging
her body to commit a final action.

Without feeling the weight
of horror, I took aim and shot.
Below shoulder, a spout of gore.
The bear then slumped to earth.

In the brewing of after-thought,
panic took hold; I fumbled
with the flick-blade, stripping
hide from too-human limbs.

The knife edge caught at knots
that mapped out a private history
of parasitism, terrain of under-skin
burrowing. Her strong scent clung
to me as I worked.

                She'd packed
on winter fat, but now she'd fill
our pots over winter months,
passing her existence into mine.

Summer Moths

By day, lie flat against the bark
of poplar with your camouflage:
ragged ashen sheets over skin,
peppered husks with ermine dots
mimicking the eyes of hawks.

By night, sweep forward delta
of wing and take flight in shadow.
Depart among drifts that float
down Rocky Mountain roads —
squalls of fat, wet snow flakes.

Do not be lured East by false
light of oil rig flares on the plain.
In seeking to tangent with blaze,
avoid the soft flutter of owl-wing.

Be true, unerring, find your way
to cover the face of zaftig moon
with clustering, courting night-flight.

As I lie beside summer's girl,
let your plump bodies, sap heavy
with ovum and sperm, thump
against the screen door, leaving
your telltale prints of fairy-dust.

In the City

Out of broken concrete, slinking,
the silken rush of body appears
between bull-rushes and shore.

Not a muskrat nosing around
in brown clay for a cheap meal,
but a rarity along urban streams:

a nut-brown mink, whose pert eyes
eclipse the water-bright sun before
she leaves with her animal speed.

Tessellated Coil

Seeking the old trickery, illusion,
and chimeric hustle that this carnal
world has puzzled, we've come
to where waves run onto shore
to reiterate designs geometric
with periodicity of Moroccan tile.

Remember the shock of python
when it wrapped around forearm
with twists and coils of serpentine
leaf-litter camouflage? Your eyes
ate up that tessellated coil of over-
lapping scale, the rhythmic plaiting
of spear heads and tear drops.

Will this pleasure in pattern recognition,
be misread by future machine intellect?
Will it find satisfaction only in abstraction,
in the collapse of quilt-work to formula?

The Wayward Season

A choke-cherry bends towards light,
seeking out space for growth.
This year, unruly lateral shoots
thrust into shadows over acidic soil.

The predation of night scavengers
scars limbs and boughs, a curling
bud mocks dry, barren branches.

Last spring, you could put ear to it,
like some *habitant* on the Saguenay,
and hear the sugary running of sap.

Are the fruitless variations of spring
without number? Do they pattern out
our rootless desires, our idiot fury?

While hands barely touched
under the bar table in Portland
the undertow tugged and pulled
like charged iron to useless scrap.
We leaned close but shot clear,
fearful of that wayward touch.

Afterglow

The room buzzes, but the band
has left; they're all played out.

The minor damage inflicted,
the echo will take days to fade.

In the blast of fluorescent light,
shadows reform guises of stain.

With barman's last call, die-hards
gather to discuss what's next —

not looking for love as much as
a lift, for it's forty below outside.

You know the woman at the bar,
a man's arm slung around waist.

Hunger lingers, prickles flesh;
you condemn yourself for this.

So what? Who hasn't been betrayed
by casual, chance acts of sex?

Turn away, down that beer, ignore stares
of the skins roosting along pool-table.

Open the side door and walk out into
titanium glare of street-lamp on ice.

Tidal Pools

1.

Rust spreads season to season;
it spreads along the rotten chassis
— a blossoming of red corrosion,
until with a gentle nudge
it gives way and becomes a hole.

2.

A clump of hair rests on
the threshold of a doorway,
announcing the loss of body
in this hotel of slow dying.

On the floor of careful finality,
a man cannot raise himself
from his bed of odor
without the hands of others.

3.

The face in the mirror,
disown it how you may,
thoughtful now, knowing.

The tide is coming in,
it is always rushing in.

Winter Bait

When squirrels sound off,
I know I have been spotted.
Perhaps they're wise, for I preyed
on them in past, gathering bait
for stepfather's traps. The stripping
of their small bodies wasn't worth
what they brought in. Still, we did it.

With a steady, gentle force
their coats would peel off.
Their flesh placed in a bucket
to ripen. That stink helped mask
smell of steel spring and jaw —
a lure for the winter sleek to
fatal snap and skinner's knife.

Caprices

Street Scene
Caught up in cold, pelting rain,
she raised a knee to hold her bag
as she knotted broken straps.

How inappropriate and dumbfounding
the urgent longing that the open curve
of calf and upraised hip brings.

Land of Thirst
Let your kisses crack open
like watermelon sowed
with the salt of your body.

A Question
A young wife's complaint,
      in the words of the English ballad:
            My Little Lamb, my sapless Man.

Will it come to that?

The Cull

Charlie B. points a finger
at the fly-blown carcass
that floats in roadside ditch.
The hunt for feral dogs has begun:
all curs, fleabags, and loose
hounds destroyed as dangerous.
A pack of strays pulled down
a boy crossing an empty lot.

We watch as the Linklater boys
wheel up and down the main drag
in a jacked-up Chevy Suburban.
They've chained a bitch in heat
to the truck's bed, and plug
any mutt that catches her whiff.

At town dump, bears work over
a mound of burnt carcasses.
Shaggy with scar across lip,
pulls the whites of intestines
from blackened Husky-flesh
with the long flash of canine.

Near the base of funeral pyre,
a cream-faced mongrel curses me
with devil-doll eyes, an all-season
radial slung around neck.

The Darker Half

He shall rise and on the surface die
  ~ Tennyson's "The Kraken"

In the deepest, darkest inky basin,
a sleeper dreaming and still awaiting.

Below regions of twilight and ash,
glamour is born on phosphor charge.
Here lives the root of Kraken legend,
colossal bane of our breathing world.
In these spare waters, dwells —
reciprocal, antipodal — our darker half,
our left hand — sinister, forgotten, shadow-
bound. The multiform, millennial gods
of Hindustan tease us with fore-
taste of the awful articulation
that stimulates tendril plague.

When fires alight and leave cities
in dust, she shall not awaken
but slumber her dark world to life.

Clay Mask

Mother was a shaper of clay.
She knew the uses of the wheel
to spin rough earth into things
of charm.
          She became angry
with the lake-woman
for drawing a portrait
that jarred.

Mother countered
with a stone-ware mask.
In the heat of the kiln,
features twisted.
                      She
glazed the mask jade-green.
With second-firing, it became
the slick face of a drowned boy.

Castor

Trappers fade the tang of metal
by rubbing the balls of beavers
over traps.
                        This is the secret lure
of Chanel N° 5 — our little deaths
in accord with the musky scent
that draws ermine to the clamp
of conibear, that perfect, poised
square, that deadly guillotine.

Imagine the stones hanging
on Castoroides.

What night beasts we might lure
with a pair of those.

Nesting Ground

Warm from mother's down,
a small mottled egg rests
in the palm of hand.

Through the lake's glare,
terns wheel and drop.
Thin wings brush us,
we ignore their threats.

The gleaning is easy
on an island colony
free from other predators.

Back at camp, a dozen
sizzle in the fry pan.
A half-formed beak
rises out of albumen,
and mother rushes out
of the tent. It's morning
and she's sick again.

Vultures at play over Mt. Norwottuck

As I climb the trail marked with white
blazes, semi-automatic fire crackles
through woods — Americans preparing
for this war or the next.
                                        At the top,
two vultures, stiff-winged, spiral
and ascend, two black t-shirts caught
in a slow-motion spin cycle.
                                        One hunches
and drops its shadow onto the canopy
below.
            As it disappears into distance,
a fixed-wing glider shoots overhead
as if *Pocom-tuck* figure of oracular
man with impossibly thin arms
had peeled off side of canyon wall
to sail across valley.
                                        On an outcrop
of basalt, a ham radio enthusiast
curses borealis, curses solar flare
for his lack of connection.
                                        He adjusts
the whip of his 20-foot antennae
and tries again, the repeated lines
of code disappearing into distortion.

We are all here, under the sun
before it burns us out, incinerates
our every word.

Wild Geese

As they fly North, they're calling.
Their sound hammers the land
from above. Eager to ease
the travail of their journey,
they seek wings to work
their wedge and ride point.
They don't know that I can't
join them in the pale blue air.

Dry Island Buffalo Jump

In the place of broken scapula,
of femur, tibia, scattered and thrown,
a bone-garden for the Blackfoot,
we found three coyote mounds,
hills steep, round, and hard packed
by the continual pounding of paws.

Beside a thicket of greasewood,
Cora laid down on an Indian blanket
thrown over brittle grass and sage.
Flipping over and putting her palms
to the diamonds of cotton weave,
she parted legs, arched her back,
took the seductive pose of cobra.
That dry, bone dust feeling left,
and we rubbed ourselves raw,
rough thighs against smooth.

Lying still on our naked sides,
we listened for the swift patter
of night beasts in their tunnels.
Only the sound of the turbid river,
new risen with mountain runoff,
echoed off coulee and ridge
behind our coyote hill, our dry
island of buffalo jump.

Artifact: The Microscope

Now we have tools to look into the blind spot of genesis,
to see conception in charnel of womb, contemplate how
we come into being through conjunction of ovum and spore
amid sea of near-dead, thousands of potential siblings
worn to exhaustion by their will to find a way into world,
flagellate movement diminishing to erasure.

Our fertilization is an alien, uncanny act. First forms and
expressions are unlike those that later materialize. As surely
as moth or butterfly, we come of chrysalis, transformation,
and cellular metamorphosis. When head crowns like the
splitting open of ripe fruit, we spill into our lives clothed in
hominid mimicry of dryad and nymph.

Van Leeuwenhoek's first act of microscopy was to observe
his own seed. Imagine the shock. Where were the legions
of microform homunculae, fully formed little men, each wrapped
in endosperm, cosmonauts within space capsules? There was
no sign of these nuts of flesh conceived to crack-down on moist
inner earth of woman, open, and grow into child. How could he
respond to the full moment of new, to the sharply expanded
range of human sense?

The Tree of Life: Palais des Papes, Avignon

In the courtyard, workmen sweat in the heat
as they raise the creator's erection: "The Tree of Life!"
It's half-way up and they're running out of time.
The bearded, greying artist, self-styled embodiment
of *neue wilde,* gesticulates and barks commands.

Builders' tools and the naked torsos
of stainless steel women litter the grass.
The ladies wait to be bolted to branches
of the metal tree — each figure anticipating
the rough touch of workers' hands when
they come to rip off coats of cellophane.

Inside, in cool rooms of musty stone,
are the artist's expressive ecstasies
of all he thinks crude, primitive, primal.

A woman in a yellow dress snorts a half-laugh
as she spies the enormity of dancer's phallus.
Behind them, anti-popes stare indifferently.
They take it all in, seen it all before.

Avocado as Evolutionary Anachronism

Ahuaqatl, in ancient Aztec tongue,
signifying testicle. The uncanny twins
of our organs of bodily generation,
those blackened, wizened *cohoñes*
that grow distorted and monstrous
in nature's swampy, florid mirror.

Rugged, knobby stone of earth,
who would imagine what butter
resides within your hardened rind?
When split, the tear-shaped fruit
reveals a core ringed with halos
of oily flesh the hue of ripe lemon
that shades to penumbra of lime.

In the lingering dark of January,
we'd pierce the knot of your seed
with wooden spits and install you
on the sill in a water-filled mason.
Your hard pit would crack open,
and feathery tendrils of red-root
would sprout and crawl the smooth,
sterile sides of translucid glass.

Kin of cinnamon, camphor and bay,
your fruit still ripens as love-song
for departed elephantine Gomphothere,
who once raised four points of tusk
and saxophoned out lamentation
over swampy coves of Vera Cruz.

Reduced to manhandling, cultivation,
to blithe, inept fosterage, and faced with
an ever-receding horizon of reduction,
and yet each vital fruit grown still exalts
your carnal twin, extinct sower of seed.

Rice Lake Serpent Mound

Two hundred feet from tip to tail,
the serpent bulges, gut bursting
to slowly grind its feast of bone.
The dead honey-comb and clog
this effigy's digestive organs;
they sit, resting chins on knees,
awaiting future, lifelessly patient.

Some wrapped in blankets of bark,
others posed with gestures of life —
they reach out to caress the cheeks
of husbands, wives, and daughters.

True to kind, the clutch-bound snake
opens wide to dislocate bony jaws,
a yawn broad enough to swallow
the ovum as if it were the earth.

Inside this ersatz egg's shell of clay,
more dead are folded-up like fetuses.
One holds silver pipes we've named for Pan,
the argent ore mined far up the Ottawa.

When will this piper play his tune
and wake these late-sleeping dead —
crack open the spell that forgetfulness
lay on the lost and buried peoples
of Cahokia, Adena, and Hopewell?

When will that child, hearing the call,
reach down and pick up her marbles,
the ones that she had thought lost,
and begin to play once again, fingering
over interlocked designs of tadpole
and frog, eye and sun, claws and palm?

Notes

p.10 *Extinct Americana: Miracinonyx, The American Cheetah.* The American Cheetah became extinct 10,000 to 12,000 years ago.

p.20 *The 401 Series.* Ontario Highway 401 as it passes through Toronto is North America's busiest highway; during peak hours it averages over 500,000 cars in transit. It widens at Pearson International Airport to 18 lanes of traffic in 4 carriageways.

p.25 *Anne Greene: 1650, Oxford.* Anne Greene was convicted of infanticide after giving birth to a still-born child. Her accuser, who was her master and the grandfather of the man who had impregnated her, died shortly after her astonishing recovery and subsequent judicial pardon. This case is described in detail in the pamphlet, *Newes from the Dead, or a True and Exact Narration of the Miraculous Deliverance of Anne Greene* (Oxford, 1651).

p.27 *Chief Snake's Funeral Catalogue.* In 1792, five soldiers of the Cameronian Regiment of Foot murdered Chief Snake in Kingston, Ontario. Originally formed by the Lords of the Convention (followers of the Presbyterian zealot, Richard Cameron), the regiment reflected its religious foundation with the regulation that each company of sixty soldiers have an appointed spiritual elder.

As Chief Snake's funeral list is non-extant, this list is a composite of similar disbursements in Upper Canada at the time.

p.30 *The Sanitarium Garden.* Vincent Van Gogh admitted himself into the Saint Paul asylum at St. Remy in May of 1889 and was released in May 1890. One of the paintings he made during his residence was "The Garden of the St.Paul Hospital."

p.33 *The Cheddar Gorge Skulls.* In 2011, Dr Silvio Bello reported that analysis of 14,700 yr. old human remains found in Gough's cave in Somerset revealed the first evidence of ritual killing in Britain. Three humans appear to have been killed, eaten, and their skulls crafted into cups or bowls.

p.36 *Big Rock (Okotoks, Alberta).* The legend of Napi and the rolling rock was offered by the Blackfoot to George Bird Grinnel, who first recorded a version of it in *Blackfoot Lodge Tales* (1892). There are many variations of the tale, often with significant differences, for as elders once told Stan Knowlton, "stories are like grass."

p.40 *Bitterskin's Curse.* The HMS Speedy sunk off Presqu'ile Point October 8, 1804 with the loss of all hands. The dead included many prominent members of the York settlement along with the accused prisoner Ogetonicut, who was survived by his mother, Bitterskin. Two young children also died, sent by parents too broke to accompany their children on the voyage.

p.44 *Pinhole Man.* At Pinhole Cave, Derbyshire, England, an engraving of a human figure on a wooly rhinoceros bone was found in the 1920's. The bone is dated to the Late Upper Paleolithic, nearly 12,000 years old. (British Museum, Palart 854).

p.48 *Peregrine.* The Highlevel bridge in Edmonton crosses the North Saskatchewan river. The vertical drop from the walkway measures 164 feet. There are currently 8 nesting pairs of peregrines in the city of Edmonton. In 1970 there was only a single nesting pair in the entire province.

p.54 *Keewatin.* Keewatin translated from Swampy Cree means blizzard.

p.59 *Tessellated Coil.* Tessellation: the repetition of interlocking geometric shapes or designs.

p.68 *Castor.* Castoroides was an extinct genus of giant beavers that lived in Northern America during the late Pleistocene era. They measured over 2.2 meters in length.

p.70 *Vultures at play over Mt. Norwottuck.* The *Pocomtuck* were the original inhabitants of the upper Connecticut valley. Through the influx of smallpox, the incursions of the Mohawk, the wars of the colonial powers of the French, English, and Dutch, they were greatly reduced in numbers and survivors fled north to join with the Abinaki peoples of Northern Vermont, New Hampshire, and Quebec.

p.75 *Avocado as Evolutionary Anachronism.* One of the Avocado's extinct seed distributors, the elephant-like Gomphothere species, survived in Mexico and Central America right up to the end of the Pleistocene (12,000 to 8,000 years ago).

p.76 *Rice Lake Serpent Mound.* Located 26 km south of Peterborough, Ontario on the shores of Rice Lake, the serpent burial mound is an earthwork built by the peoples of the Hopewellian/ Point Peninsula culture sometime between 50BCE to 300CE. Unlike other indigenous groups of our continent, these people played the mouth organ (a.k.a. pan pipes).

Acknowledgements

"Avocado as Evolutionary Anachronism" appeared in *The Fiddlehead*. "The Cull" first appeared in *The Antigonish Review*. "Homecoming" and "Riverbank" appeared in *ByWords*. "Tidal Pools" and "The Sanitarium Garden" appeared in *Ottawater*. "Reclamation" first appeared in *The Dalhousie Review*. "Crush" appeared in *Steel Chisel*. "Skyline" appeared in *Inwords Magazine*. "Peregrine" appeared as one of Michel Pleau's Parliamentary Poet Laureate Poem of the Month choices. "The 401 Series," "Tree Lobster," and "The Tree of Life: Palais des Papes, Avignon" appeared in Tree Reading Series' Hot Ottawa Voices Podcast. An earlier version of "Artifact: The Levellois Point" was shortlisted for *Vallum*'s Poetry Award, 2015.

Thanks to my editor, Micheline Maylor, for her insight and perception. Thanks to the community of writers in Ottawa, including, but not limited to Monty Reid, Sneha Madhavan-Reese, Stephen Brockwell, Vivian Vavassis, Armand Garnet Ruffo, Deanna Young, David O'Meara, Matt Jones, rob mclennan, and Frances Boyle. Thanks to Tree Reading series, VERSe Ottawa, and the small press book fair. Thanks to the writers and organizers at Sage Hill and Juniper. Thanks also to Zachary Schomburg. Thanks to Robert Kroetsch, who helped plant the seed. Thanks especially to Don McKay for his encouragement and mentorship.